Country File
China

Michael March

FRANKLIN WATTS
LONDON • SYDNEY

First published in 2003 by
Franklin Watts
96 Leonard Street, London
EC2A 4XD

Franklin Watts Australia
45-51 Huntley Street,
Alexandria, NSW 2015

COUNTRY FILE: CHINA produced for Franklin Watts by
Bender Richardson White, PO Box 266, Uxbridge, UK.
Editor: Lionel Bender
Designer and Page Make-up: Ben White
Picture Researcher: Cathy Stastny
Cover Make-up: Mike Pilley, Radius
Production: Kim Richardson

Graphics and Maps: Stefan Chabluk

Consultant: Dr Terry Jennings, a former geography teacher
and university lecturer. He is now a full-time writer of
children's geography and science books.

A CIP catalogue record for this book is available
from the British Library.

ISBN 0-7496-4815-5

Manufactured in China

Picture Credits

Pages 1: Eye Ubiquitous/Julia Waterlow. 3: PhotoDisc
Inc/John Dakers/Life File. 4: Eye Ubiquitous/Chris
Fairclough. 6: Eye Ubiquitous/Julia Waterlow.
7: PhotoDisc Inc/Neil Beer. 8: Eye Ubiquitous/Julia
Waterlow. 10: Eye Ubiquitous/Julia Waterlow. 11: Eye
Ubiquitous/Julia Waterlow. 12: Eye Ubiquitous/Julia
Waterlow. 15: James Davis Travel Photography. 16: Eye
Ubiquitous/P.M.Field. 17: Corbis Images/Lui Liqun.
18: Eye Ubiquitous/Chris Fairclough. 19: Corbis
Images/Liu Liqun. 20: Eye Ubiquitous/Sean Aidan.
21: Eye Ubiquitous/Chris Fairclough. 22: Eye
Ubiquitous/Julia Waterlow. 23: Eye Ubiquitous/Julia
Waterlow. 24: Eye Ubiquitous/John Hulme. 26: Eye
Ubiquitous/Geoff Daniels. 28: Eye Ubiquitous/Chris
Fairclough. 30: PhotoDisc Inc/Glen Allison.
31: PhotoDisc Inc/ Glen Allison.

Cover Photo: Eye Ubiquitous/Geoff Daniels.

Spelling of proper names
This book uses widely accepted forms of modern
Chinese names. In other books, you may find
alternative spellings for names, for example, Beijing
(Peking), Chiangjiang (Chiang-jiang or Yangtze-Kiang),
Huang He (Yellow River), Guangzhou (Canton),
Chongqing (Chungking), Mao Zedong (Mao Tse-tung).

The Author
Michael March is a full-time writer and
editor of non-fiction books. He has
written more than 15 books for children
about different countries of the world.

Contents

Welcome to China

The People's Republic of China is one of the biggest countries in the world. It spreads across much of East Asia, covering one-fifth of the Earth's land mass.

China has fourteen neighbouring countries, including India and Russia, and most of its eastern boundary overlooks the Pacific Ocean. Its borders stretch for more than 40,000 kilometres, of which over 18,000 kilometres is coastline dotted with islands. Nearly two-thirds of the country consists of mountains or hills.

Oldest civilization

Nine-tenths of the people living in China are ethnic Chinese, or Han. The Chinese have one of the world's oldest civilizations, with a written language going back 6,000 years. Paper and printing, the compass, gunpowder, porcelain, silk and canal locks are some of the things that were invented or discovered in China and later introduced to the rest of the world.

The Great Wall

One of the world's most famous landmarks is the Great Wall of China. Measuring 6,000 km in length, it was built in ancient times to keep out invaders from the north. The wall rises to 16 m at its highest and is about 7 m wide. Part of the Great Wall is shown on the cover of this book.

In Shanghai, people walk alongside the Huangpu River. The waterfront area known as the Bund and the old city nearby are tourist attractions. ▼

The Land

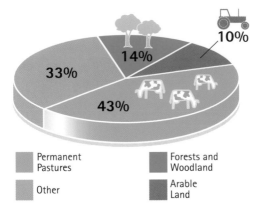

10%

14%

33%

43%

Permanent Pastures

Other

Forests and Woodland

Arable Land

Chinas vastness makes for a wide variety of landscapes: from stony deserts, snow-capped mountains and grasslands to fertile valleys and tropical rainforests.

In China, climates, too, vary greatly from region to region. The far north-east has no distinct summer, the far south no real winter. The south-east coast gets more than thirty times as much rain as the dry north-west.

In south-western China, the Plateau of Tibet is known as 'the roof of the world' because it is so wide and so high. Here, in this highland wilderness, China's longest river, the mighty Changjiang (or Yangtse) starts its 6,300-kilometre journey to the East China Sea. South of the plateau, Mount Everest straddles China's border with Nepal. Rising to 8,848 metres, Qomolangma, as the Chinese call it, is the world's highest peak. China has five main mountain ranges and more than 50,000 rivers.

▲ For its vast size, China has relatively little land suitable for crop cultivation. Much more of the terrain is grazing land.

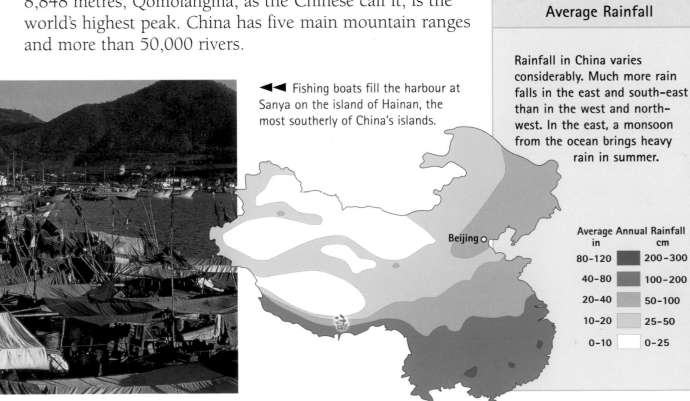

◄◄ Fishing boats fill the harbour at Sanya on the island of Hainan, the most southerly of China's islands.

Beijing o

Average Rainfall

Rainfall in China varies considerably. Much more rain falls in the east and south-east than in the west and north-west. In the east, a monsoon from the ocean brings heavy rain in summer.

Average Annual Rainfall	
in	cm
80–120	200–300
40–80	100–200
20–40	50–100
10–20	25–50
0–10	0–25

Deserts and monsoons

Northern China contains two great deserts – the Taklimakan in the north-west, and the Gobi on the Mongolian plateau. The plains of north-eastern and eastern China have the biggest cities, including the capital Beijing, as well as some of the richest farming land.

These lowland regions are watered by the Huang He (Yellow River) and Changjiang. The Huang He is known as 'China's sorrow' because, over the centuries, many people have drowned when the river burst its banks. The Changjiang has also been prone to flooding and in 1998 claimed 4,000 lives. Other natural hazards that China faces include droughts, earthquakes and typhoons – spiralling, tropical rainstorms that can strike the coast and do great damage.

Plants and Animals

China's rich plant life includes oak, ash, elm, peony, chrysanthemum, camellia, lotus, ginseng, peach tree and many other species.

The north-eastern forests of fir, larch, spruce and pine are home to sable, moose and the very rare Manchurian tiger. Wild yaks and a few snow leopards roam the Tibetan plateau. Giant pandas live in the bamboo forests of the south-west. Gibbons, macaques and other monkey species inhabit the broadleaf evergreen and palm forests of the tropical south.

◄◄ Huge outcrops of rock surround the flat plain of the Xijiang River in southern China, near the border with Vietnam. Here, summers are long and warm and winters generally mild.

Web Search ►►

► http://www.chinatoday.com/general/a.htm
General information including climate and geography from China Today magazine.

► http://china.9c9c.com/Geography/
Link to pages on geography and climate.

The People

About 1.29 billion (1,290 million) people live in China – more than in any other country. On average, one in every five people in the world is Chinese. Some 92 per cent of China's population are Han, or ethnic Chinese. The rest belong to 55 other ethnic or cultural groups.

The Han are descended from the many tribes that long ago settled the plains of eastern China. Later generations built great cities and empires. Another famous people, the Mongols, ruled the country some 700 years ago as part of the biggest empire the world has ever seen. Today some 5 million Mongols live in northern China. Other ethnic groups, such as the 7 million Uygurs of the north-west and the Tibetans (2.6 million), came under Chinese rule as China expanded its borders westward.

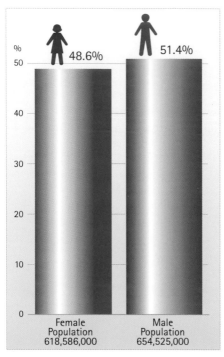

Female Population 618,586,000	Male Population 654,525,000

▲ Males outnumber females in every age group up to 65. Over 65, there are fewer men than women.

Life expectancy is high but less than in most western countries. On average, females live longer. ▼

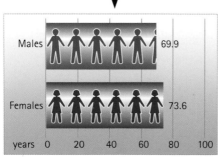

◄◄ A street scene in Bijie in Guizhou Province, southern China. Here live such ethnic groups as the Miao, Dong, and Zhuang.

Chinese language

Chinese has no alphabet, in which individual letters represent separate sounds. Instead picture-like characters, or symbols, represent words or ideas. There are some 50,000 of these characters. The written language is the same all over China, but the spoken language has seven main dialects, including Yue (Cantonese). The official spoken language is the northern Chinese dialect, as used in the capital city, Beijing. It is known as *Putonghua* (meaning 'standard speech') or Mandarin Chinese.

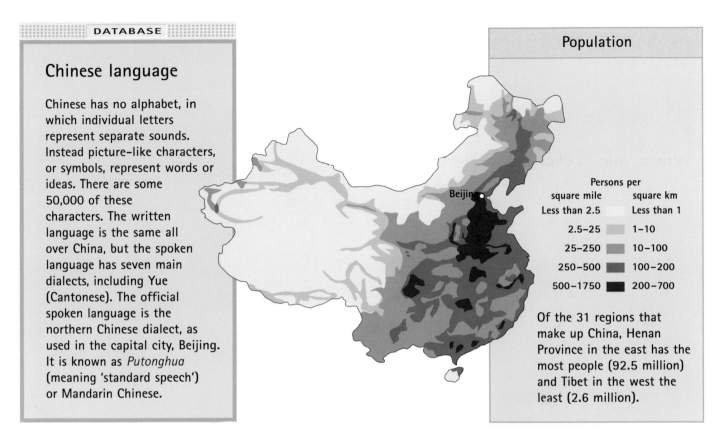

Population

Beijing

Persons per	
square mile	square km
Less than 2.5	Less than 1
2.5–25	1–10
25–250	10–100
250–500	100–200
500–1750	200–700

Of the 31 regions that make up China, Henan Province in the east has the most people (92.5 million) and Tibet in the west the least (2.6 million).

National minorities

The biggest of the ethnic groups – or nationalities, as they often are called – are the Zhuang of south-western China, who number some 15 million. Many of these national minorities have their own languages. The Uygurs, for example, speak a language that is distantly related to Turkish. But everyone also learns Mandarin Chinese (*Putonghua*), which is China's official language.

Population age

About a quarter of all the people living in China are aged 14 or younger, and about 7 per cent are 65 or above. Between 1990 and 2000, the year of the latest population census, the numbers in the youngest age group fell by nearly 5 per cent. Over the same period, there was a 1.4 per cent rise in the numbers of those aged 65 and over. On average, 64 out of every 10 million people live beyond the age of 100.

Web Search ▶▶

▶ http://www.chinatoday.com/people/people.html
Gives information on population, birth rates, age groups in China.

▶ http://china.9c9c.com/Culture/Minorities/topic_237.html
Chinese website giving history of cultural minorities.

▶ http://www.stats.gov.cn/english/index.htm
Website of China's National Bureau of Statistics.

Urban and Rural Life

In 1982, China's population topped 1 billion for the first time. Since then, the number of people has risen by some 290 million, but the average rate of increase per year has slowed to about one per cent. Some two-thirds of the population live in rural areas, although more and more people are now moving to the towns and cities.

In the past ten years or so, the proportion of city dwellers has grown from about a quarter to nearly a third. Most of the big cities, such as the capital Beijing, which has nearly 14 million people, and Shanghai (17 million), are in the densely populated eastern half of the country. In the western half, no city has more than 1 million people. Many of the national minorities live in western or southern China or near the borders.

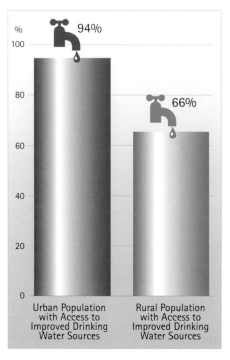

▲ Overall, 75 per cent of China's people have access to improved drinking water sources, but with a better service for urban than for rural areas. Sources of drinking water range from taps in houses and public standpipes to boreholes, wells and protected springs.

◄◄ A village on the plains of northern China, where traditional life goes on and people still use animal-drawn vehicles.

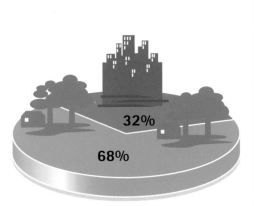

■ Percentage of Population Living in Urban Areas

■ Percentage of Population Living in Rural Areas

32%

68%

▲ Twice as many people live in rural areas as in the towns and cities, although the pattern of settlement is slowly changing.

▲ Shops, traffic and people fill the streets of Shenzhen, a large modern town near Hong Kong.

Chinese houses

Traditionally, houses in towns and cities such as Beijing were built around a square courtyard. The house belonging to the head of the family faced south, the most favourable direction according to the ancient Chinese art of Feng Shui.

Today, in Beijing and across China, traditional houses are increasingly giving way to high-rise buildings. In distant Tibet, new, multi-storey flats are appearing alongside old wood and stone blockhouses, where animals occupy the ground floor and the family lives above. Farther north on the steppe, or grasslands, the Mongols once lived in circular tents called yurts. They herded sheep and goats and moved around from pasture to pasture on horseback. Nowadays many of them are settled, live in wood and brick houses and work on farms or in factories.

Web Search ►►

► http://china.9c9c.com/ Arts/Architecture/
Survey of architectural styles across China.

► http://www.un.org/ Depts/unsd/social/ watsan.htm#wat
UN site with data on water supply and sanitation worldwide.

Farming and Fishing

Rice and wheat have been grown in China for thousands of years. Today, these are still the main food crops. Fish farming was practised in ancient China. Now it accounts for more than half the country's annual fish catch, which is by far the biggest in the world.

Only about one-tenth of the land can be used for agriculture, which provides work for half of China's working population. Most farms are small and family-run, replacing the earlier, much larger, communally run collective farms. The farms are efficient and productive: currently China is the world's leading producer of rice and wheat as well as maize and several other crops.

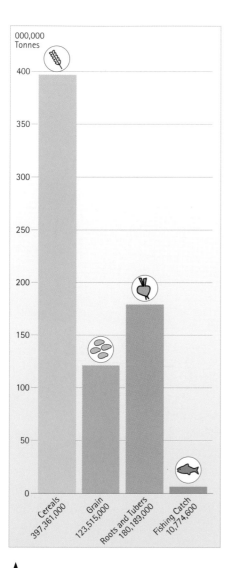

000,000
Tonnes

Cereals 397,361,000	
Grain 123,515,000	
Roots and Tubers 180,183,000	
Fishing Catch 10,774,600	

▲▲ Production of cereal crops – mostly rice, wheat, maize – far outweighs other grains (such as buckwheat) or roots and tubers, of which sweet potatoes are the most important.

In some parts of China, rice is grown on artificial terraces with walls that trap rainwater. ▶▶

Increased Production

In China today, some farmers have tractors, and the use of farm machinery is increasing. However, much of the work is still done using hand tools. Extensive irrigation, new seed varieties and the greater use of fertilizers have allowed some farmers to harvest two or more crops a year on the same land.

■ Pasture
■ Cropland
■ Forest
■ Mountain Region
■ Desert

Beijing

Farming

🐂 Cattle
🐖 Pigs
🐐 Goats
🐑 Sheep
○ Melons
🌴 Oases
🌾 Cereals
🌽 Corn (Maize)
☁ Cotton
🐟 Fishing
 Peanuts
🍇 Grapes
○ Rice
▦ Sugar Cane
 Tea
 Soya Beans
 Sugar Beet

Rice is the main crop in eastern China. Wheat and maize are grown farther north. Cotton and grapes are grown in the north-west. The south produces sugar cane and cattle. Sheep and goats graze the pasture areas.

A wide variety of crops

China grows more than three-quarters of the world's sweet potatoes and produces more cotton and tobacco than any other country. Other agricultural produce includes apples, melons, potatoes, carrots, peanuts, soya beans, tea, sugar cane, sugar beet, rubber, jute, hemp and silk. Sericulture – breeding silk worms for spinning silk – was invented by the Chinese. Livestock includes numerous pigs (about 40 per cent of the world's total), sheep, cattle, goats, water buffalo, horses, camels in desert regions and, in Tibet, yaks.

Fishing fleet

Many of the 250,000 or so boats that make up China's fishing fleet are small, privately operated trawlers. Hairtail, yellow croaker, Chub mackerel, herring, red snapper, cod, sardine, shark, octopus, squid and abalone are some of the 150 or so species caught in the East and South China Seas and offshore waters. Boats also catch a variety of shellfish and collect edible seaweeds. Black carp and other carp varieties raised in ponds, rivers, lakes and reservoirs form a major part of the freshwater catch.

Web Search ▶▶

▶ http://www.lib.noaa.gov/china/fishing.htm
Detailed information and tables on China's fishing industry.

▶ http://www.economist.co.uk/countries/china/
Economist *magazine website pages devoted to information on China.*

Resources and Industry

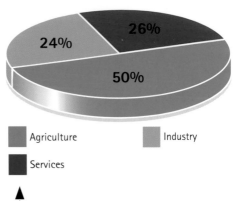

24% | 26%
50%

■ Agriculture   ■ Industry
■ Services

▲ Half of China's 730 million
workforce is made up of workers in
mining, manufacturing and the service
industries.

Industry and Resources

Shanghai, which employs about 4
million people in 40,000 industrial
works, is the biggest industrial
centre, followed by Beijing.

- 🚗 Car Manufacture
- ⚗ Chemicals
- ☄ Coal
- 💧 Oil
- ⚡ Electronics
- 🔧 Engineering
- $ Finance
- 🗋 Food Processing
- ☯ Iron and Steel
- 💉 Pharmaceuticals
- 🚢 Shipbuilding
- 👕 Textiles

China is rich in mineral resources: from coal and
oil to salt, uranium, gold, iron and many others.
Mining, engineering and manufacturing together
account for more than half the country's wealth.

All towns and most rural areas are connected to the
electricity grid, making China the world's largest electricity
producer. Most of the country's electricity power stations
run on coal. China has the biggest coal-mining industry in
the world. Much of the coal comes from Shanxi and
neighbouring provinces, north of the Changjiang River.

Coal along with oil, which China has in abundance
inland and offshore, supply about nine-tenths of the
country's power. Most of the rest comes from more than
50 large hydro-electric stations, which draw their energy
from rivers and dams. Nuclear power, using uranium as its
fuel, provides about 1 per cent of China's electricity.

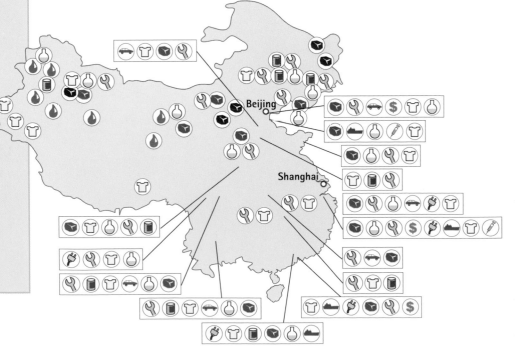

Factories and services

Across China, numerous factories turn out all kinds of products: fertilizers, cigarettes, sewing machines, machine tools, cars and motorcycles, watches, televisions, computers, mobile telephones, canned foods and other foodstuffs, shoes and clothing and much else besides. Other industries provide such services as insurance, banking and transport as well as hotels to cater for China's growing numbers of foreign tourists.

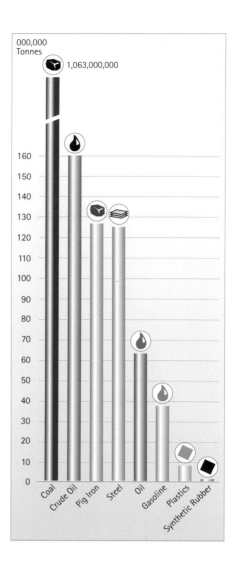

000,000 Tonnes

1,063,000,000

Coal · Crude Oil · Pig Iron · Steel · Oil · Gasoline · Plastics · Synthetic Rubber

Steel and ships

Huge deposits of iron ore have helped make China's steel industry one of the world's largest. Some 1,400 types of steel are produced, including high-class cold-rolled and zinc-plated steel. Shipbuilding is another major enterprise, with 800 or so shipyards each employing around 10,000 workers. China is now the third-largest shipbuilding nation, after Japan and South Korea.

Coal is by far the biggest of China's industrial products, followed by oil, iron and steel. ►►

In Shanghai, ferries cross the Huangpu River and ocean-going vessels are loaded with goods to transport via the East China Sea around the world. ▼

Web Search ►►

► http://www.china.org.cn/e-Internet/JJ/HTM/7-1.htm
Table showing energy production figures by type of energy source.

► www.allchinadata.com/english/industrial%20economy/table13.htm
Table showing China's industrial output by product.

Transport

Over the past 50 years, China has built up a 2.5-million-kilometre system of roads, railways, waterways and air routes that cover the length and breadth of the country.

Air China and other Chinese airlines operate on some 130 international routes while every year the 1,800-strong merchant shipping fleet carries cargo and passengers to and from 1,100 ports across the world.

Within China, about a third of all passenger and freight traffic is carried on the railways. In the east of the country, Beijing is the hub of the rail network, with lines stretching as far as Harbin in the north and Kowloon in the south. National Railways, the main rail service, has over 14,000 locomotives, of which about 1,000 are steam-driven.

░░░░░░░░ DATABASE ░░░░░░░░

Urban transport

Buses run in all towns and cities, some of which also have private minibuses. Beijing, Shanghai and Hong Kong operate fast, efficient subway trains. Taxis, motorcycle taxis and motorized or bicycle rickshaws offer other ways of getting around. Bicycles have long been a popular means of transport, and about one in four Chinese owns one.

In cities, most people get around on bicycles or buses.

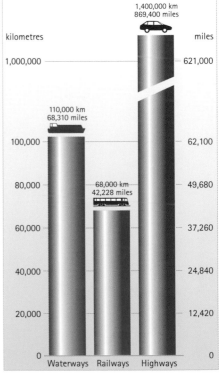

kilometres — miles

	1,400,000 km / 869,400 miles
1,000,000	621,000
110,000 km / 68,310 miles	
100,000	62,100
80,000	68,000 km / 42,228 miles	49,680
60,000	37,260
40,000	24,840
20,000	12,420
0	0
Waterways Railways Highways	

The comparative length of China's waterway, rail and road systems. ▶▶

Waterways, roads and airports

Waterways account for more than half of all freight movements. Barges, junks and steamers can sail up the Changjiang River as far as Chongqing, and many other major rivers, too, are navigable. The 2,000-year-old Grand Canal, which runs southward from Beijing to Hangzhou, is also still much used today. More than 64 million people and a billion tonnes of cargo pass through Shanghai, Guangzhou (Canton) and other seaports every year.

A vast road network includes 9,000 kilometres of motorways connecting the big towns. In a year, some 13 billion people travel by road, and lorries transport some 970 million tonnes of freight.

China's international airlines serve cities as far apart as Tokyo and Vancouver. Some 800 aircraft fly from 140 Chinese airports to destinations within China and beyond. They carry 60 million passengers a total distance of 1.5 million kilometres on 1,100 air routes in a year.

▲ Urban freeways form part of the transport links of modern Shanghai.

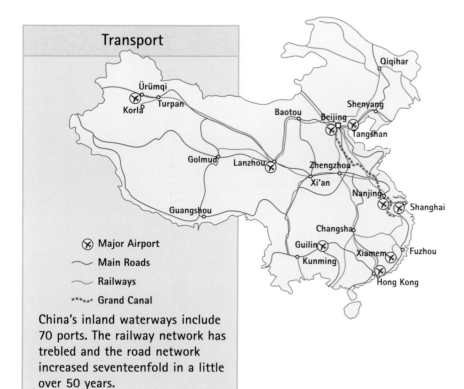

Transport

Qiqihar
Ürümqi
Korla Turpan
Baotou Shenyang
Beijing Tangshan
Golmud Lanzhou Zhengzhou
Xi'an
Nanjing
Guangshou Shanghai
Changsha
Guilin
Xiamem Fuzhou
Kunming
Hong Kong

⊗ Major Airport
⌢ Main Roads
⌢ Railways
•••• Grand Canal

China's inland waterways include 70 ports. The railway network has trebled and the road network increased seventeenfold in a little over 50 years.

🌐 **Web Search** ►►

► http://www.china.org.cn/e-Internet/JJ/HTM/jjindex.htm
Chinese website with links to data and tables on transport, employment and economics.

► http://www.air-china.co.uk/
British website for Air China airlines.

Education

Children in China must attend school for at least nine years. After that, if they pass an examination they can continue their studies for another three years. They can then apply to go to university or technical college, but competition for places is very fierce.

At age 6 or 7, children start primary school, where they usually spend six years, before moving on to junior secondary school for a further three years. They study Chinese language, mathematics, music, science, painting, history, geography, physical education and, later, English and other foreign languages.

From the beginning, they also learn moral education. This teaches them to love their country, respect the law, value knowledge and behave as a responsible member of society. Children attend classes from Monday to Friday and schools often require them to wear school uniforms.

China began its adult literacy programme more than 50 years ago. Today the vast majority of the population of all ages can read and write. ▼

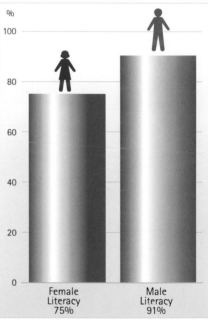

Female Literacy 75% Male Literacy 91%

◄◄ In a primary school in Xi'an, the capital of Shaanxi Province, children read at their desks with the teacher. The school year is divided into two terms, lasting a total of 38 or 39 weeks.

A variety of schools

In the cities, many children progress from junior to senior middle school to extend their education till they are 18 or 19. To do so, they first must pass an examination set by the local authority. Some schools in the capital, Beijing, and other big cities are 'key schools', which offer the best education and accept only the most academically able students. Some schools are vocational or technical, providing training in farming, engineering or other trades.

University places

On graduating from secondary school, students may try to gain entry to one of the thousand or so universities or technical colleges by sitting an entrance examination. However, many do not succeed, as there are far fewer places available than there are applicants. For every 10,000 people in China, there are less than 50 undergraduate students. Some unsuccessful applicants pursue their education through courses run by factory schools, known as 'workers' universities'.

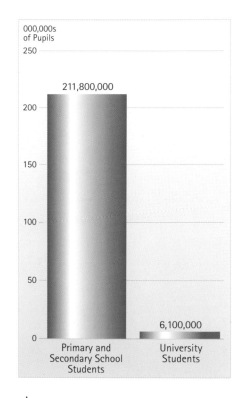

More than 85 per cent of students complete their compulsory nine years of education at primary and junior secondary school. University students make up less than 3 per cent of the total student numbers.

Students in a classroom in Beijing University. This is the most prestigious university in China. ▼▼

Web Search ►►

► http://www.edu.cn/Home
Page/english/education/
index.shtml
China Education and Research Network, giving information on all levels of education.

► http://www.china.org.cn/
e-china/education/index.
htm
Articles on all types of education with links to statistical tables.

Sport and Leisure

Physical fitness is very important to people in China, and about 300 million of them play some kind of sport regularly. Football and basketball are among the most popular team sports, with major league games drawing big crowds.

Many Chinese also enjoy traditional martial arts pursuits, such as kung fu or taijiquan, as well as canoeing, rock-climbing and other outdoor activities.

In international competitions, China is especially famous for its gymnastics and table tennis. At the Olympic Games held in 2000 in Sydney, Australia, the Chinese table tennis team made history by winning all four gold medals for a second time running.

Gymnastics is extremely popular in China. Overall, Chinese athletes rank third in the world, behind the Americans and the Russians ▼

Martial Arts

Kung fu and taijiquan are ancient Chinese martial arts based on the use of punches, kicks and open hand blows to defeat the opponent. They both include animal-like movements, such as the kung fu monkey pose, but differ from each other in their approach. Kung fu relies on building up physical strength, such as hardening the hands to break bricks. Taijiquan is based on the *qi*, or life energy, which comes from within to generate the power. Taijiquan movements practised slowly are a popular form of exercise.

Traditional sports

Many of China's national minorities have their own traditional sports and pastimes. Wrestling, archery and horseback riding are favourites among the Mongols.

In Tibet, people hold yak-racing competitions, while the Miao and other peoples of southern China have 'dragon boat' races (the boats are dragon-shaped). The Gaoshan people, in the east, love flying kites, as do many Han Chinese. The kite was invented in ancient China.

▲ In Beijing, a poster advertises the Olympic Games, to be held here in 2008.

DATABASE

Board games

The most popular board game among the Chinese is *weiqi*, or Go. It originated in China 3,000 years ago. The Chinese also have their own version of chess, called *xiangqi*. Today, conventional chess has a bigger following thanks to the success of Chinese players, especially women players, at international level. Another popular, very different game is *mah-jong*, a gambling game which, like dominoes, is played with tiles and can be very noisy.

Web Search ▶▶

▶ http://www.world stadiums.com/asia/ countries/china.shtml
Information on sports stadiums in China.

▶ http://www.china.org. cn/e-china/sports/ index.htm
Pages on sport from the Chinese website called China in Brief.

▶ http://english.people daily.com.cn/china/1999 0910A110.html
People's Daily *newspaper website giving history of sport in China.*

▶ http://www.chinatoday. com/sports/index.htm
Pages on sport and recreation from China Today *magazine website.*

Daily Life and Religion

People in China can expect to live twice as long as they did 50 years ago. Their earnings have more than trebled in a little over 20 years, so they need to spend a smaller proportion of their income on food.

However, families in towns are nearly three times better off than families living in rural areas. Less than a third of rural households has a washing machine, compared to more than nine-tenths of urban households. On average, every urban household owns at least one colour television set, while under half of all rural households have one.

The working week

Officially, people in China work a basic 40-hour week, spread over five days, with paid annual leave and days off for national holidays. Offices normally open on weekdays at 8.00 in the morning and close at 5.00 in the evening. Shops, especially in the big cities, often close much later and some open on Saturdays and on Sundays.

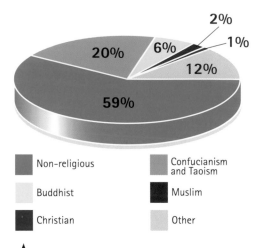

2%
1%
6%
20%
12%
59%

- Non-religious
- Buddhist
- Christian
- Confucianism and Taoism
- Muslim
- Other

▲ Religion in China. Buddhists include some Mongols, Tibetans and Han. Muslims live mostly in western China. Many Miao and Yi peoples in the south are Christians.

DATABASE

Army conscription

Men and women aged 18 to 22 can be conscripted to serve in the armed forces for two years. China's armed forces, called the People's Liberation Army (PLA), number some 3 million, most of whom are men. The PLA includes an army, called Ground Forces, nearly 2 million strong, a navy, an air force and security forces.

◄◄ A woman dictates to a professional letter-writer outside a post office in Xi'an. Writing neatly using symbols requires great skill.

Health schemes

Thanks to a massive health care programme, begun in the 1950s, many Chinese citizens are covered by health and unemployment insurance schemes, which are mostly paid for by the state. Disabled people, those on low incomes and senior citizens also receive benefits.

Religion

China has no official religion. Buddhism, Taoism and Confucianism are the traditional religions of the Han Chinese. Buddhism came to China from India nearly 2,000 years ago. Taoism and Confucianism are based on the teachings of ancient Chinese philosophers.

Almost every town and village has a street market, like this one in Chengdu, the capital of Sichuan Province. This trader is selling peas and beans. ▼

Taoism

Tao is believed to be a natural force. It has two parts, *yin* and *yang*. Yin is associated with earth, darkness, the moon and the feminine, and Yang with air, light, the sun and the masculine. The two forces are always struggling with one another, influencing the weather and a person's health.

Web Search ▶▶

▶ http://english.people daily.com.cn/china/ 19990914A119.html
Article on improvements in living standards in China.

▶ http://www.china.org. cn/e-Internet/KJ/ HTM/kindex.htm
Page with summary of progress in public heath and links to numerous tables containing health data.

▶ http://www.china.org. cn/e-china/livelihood/ socialSecurity.htm
China in Brief website article on social security provisions.

▶ http://www.chinatoday. com/arm/index.htm
Information and data about China's armed forces.

Arts and Media

Some of China's many artistic traditions, such as calligraphy – using brushstrokes to write Chinese characters – go back many centuries. Likewise, Chinese opera has a long history but is still enjoyed today alongside modern Chinese films, which have won international acclaim.

The Chinese invented paper more than 2,000 years ago, after which calligraphy, painting and poetry developed together. Artists painted on paper, using brushes dipped in ink. They added Chinese characters, or sometimes whole poems, to the scenes they had created. Today, calligraphy is still an important art in China. Another continuing ancient art is making vases in eggshell-thin porcelain.

Chinese opera

There are more than 300 forms of Chinese opera, which started 800 years ago. The most famous of these, the Beijing Opera, has been going since the 19th century. Actors in face-paint and colourful costumes sing and dance their way through musical dramas, to the accompaniment of the *pipa* (a stringed instrument like a lute), oboes, drums and gongs. Often the action on stage also includes acrobatic mock-fighting.

An entertainer finishes dressing and completes her make-up to act in a performance by the world-famous Chinese State Circus. ▼

Tourism

Tourism to China is increasing. Overseas visitors come to see China's ancient architectural wonders, such as the Imperial Palace in Beijing (as shown in the photo on page 3) and the Great Wall (shown on this book's cover), and to investigate the many riches of one of the world's oldest cultures.

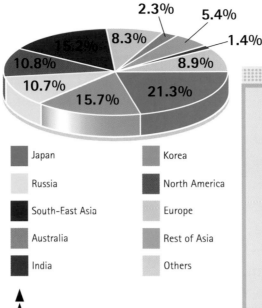

Japan

Russia

South-East Asia

Australia

India

Korea

North America

Europe

Rest of Asia

Others

▲
▲ Most of China's 11.1 million foreign tourists in a year are from neighbouring Asian countries, notably Japan and Korea. Visitors from Russia and North America both number over 1 million.

Television and radio broadcast stations. ▼
▼

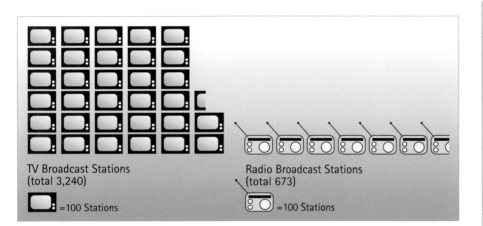

TV Broadcast Stations (total 3,240)

☐ =100 Stations

Radio Broadcast Stations (total 673)

📻 =100 Stations

Television, radio and publishing

More than a billion people watch television in China. The national broadcasting organization, China Central Television, along with some 3,000 other stations across the country and cable and satellite channels make up the world's largest television network. The national radio station transmits seven programmes whose total broadcasting time averages 130 hours a day. More than 2,000 different newspapers are published in China, and more than 186 million copies printed. About 10,000 new books appear every year.

Chinese cinema

From the 1950s, China turned out many films with a political message. In the 1980s, a new generation of film directors working in studios in the city of Xi'an made Chinese cinema famous. Film such as *Yellow Earth*, directed by Chen Kaige, and Zhang Yimou's *Red Sorghum* and *Raise the Red Lantern* won international recognition and made a star of the female actor Gong Li.

Web Search ▶▶

▶ http://china.9c9c.com/Arts/
Information on Chinese art and its history, with links to pages on opera, music, architecture and calligraphy.

▶ http://www.dianying.com/en/
Chinese movie database. All kinds of information about Chinese films, directors and actors.

▶ http://www.china.org.cn/e-china/tourism/index.htm
China in Brief pages on tourism to China, its history, sights, tourist organizations.

▶ http://www.chinatoday.com/med/a.htm
Listings of Chinese newspapers, magazines and circulation figures.

Government

The People's Republic of China is governed by the Communist Party. The Party has a pyramid-like structure, which mirrors the structure of the National People's Congress, China's national assembly body. Usually those at the top of each pyramid – the leading figures in the government and in the Communist Party – are the same people.

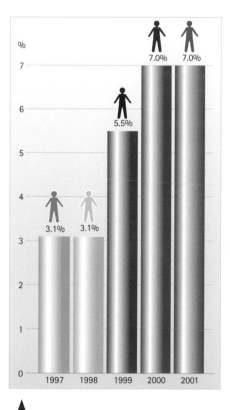

▲ Five years of unemployment figures for China. Unemployment has risen as the government has moved from a state-run economy to one that allows more private businesses.

Tiananmen Square in Beijing. In front of the great gateway to the Imperial Palace hangs a portrait of Mao Zedong, founder of the People's Republic. ▼▼

DATABASE

The Communist Party

With some 65 million members, the Chinese Communist Party is the largest political party in the world. About 20,000 members are elected by the Party to serve on the National People's Congress for five years. Congress then chooses a Central Committee, whose 350 or so members elect the Politburo (political bureau), consisting of about 20 members, its standing committee and the general secretary, who is the Party head.

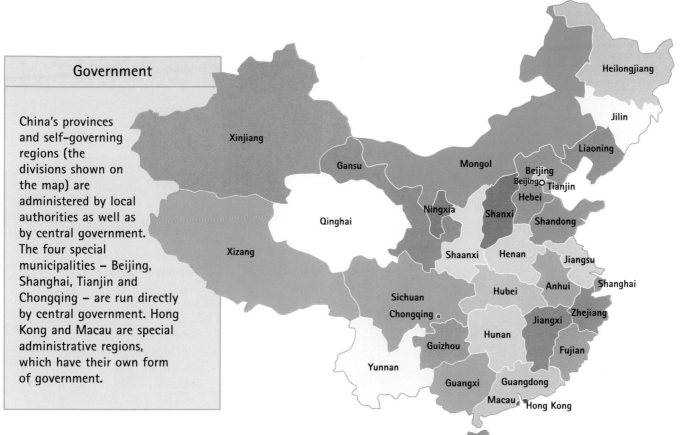

Government

China's provinces and self-governing regions (the divisions shown on the map) are administered by local authorities as well as by central government. The four special municipalities – Beijing, Shanghai, Tianjin and Chongqing – are run directly by central government. Hong Kong and Macau are special administrative regions, which have their own form of government.

The Chinese constitution

Under China's constitution, every citizen has a right to be educated, to work, to vote in elections and to stand for election. Members of the National People's Congress are elected to serve for five years. Anyone aged 18 or over may vote. The 3,000-strong Congress passes laws and approves economic plans. It chooses the country's president, which is largely a ceremonial role, as well as the prime minister, who heads the government, and the members of the State Council, or Cabinet.

Government control

Two Central Military Commissions, one for the government and one for the Communist Party, control the armed forces. Over four years, China has increased military spending by an average of 15 per cent a year. In 20 years, the amount that the government collects annually in taxes has increased some twentyfold. Businesses pay between 15 and 33 per cent tax on profits, with inland areas paying less than the richer, coastal regions.

Web Search ▶▶

▶ http://www.china.org.cn/e-china/finance/index.htm
China in Brief *pages on finance and taxation.*

▶ http://www.china.org.cn/e-china/politicalsystem/index.htm
China in Brief *pages on the political system, the constitution and government.*

▶ http://www.chinatoday.com/gov/a.htm
A who's who of government, with numerous links to information on central government agencies.

Chronology of Historical Events: 221 BCE to CE 1945

221–206 BCE
China unified under Emperor Qin Shi Huangdi

CE 1271–1368
Conquest and rule of China by the Mongols

1860
China's defeat in Second Opium War leads to the loss of Hong Kong to Britain

1911
Sun Yat-sen proclaims a republic and founds the Kuomintang political party. The child emperor Puyi abdicates

1916
Feuding warlords begin to tear the country apart

1921 Chinese Communist Party founded in Shanghai

1923
Communists join Kuomintang to fight warlords

1925
Death of Sun Yat-sen. Kuomintang now led by anti-Communist Chiang Kai-shek, who purges Communists in 1927

1931–45
Japanese invasion and occupation of China, starting with Manchuria, in north-eastern China

1934–5
Long March. Retreat by Communists covering 9,600 kilometres, to escape from Kuomintang and to regroup

1936
Kuomintang and Communists join forces against Japanese occupation forces

Place in the World

China is one of the worlds oldest civilizations. In 1911, after many centuries of rule by emperors, it became a republic, and in 1949, Mao Zedong founded the People's Republic of China. Today China is a permanent member of the United Nations Security Council and has the world's second largest economy.

During World War II (1939–45) and before, the Chinese fought both the Japanese, who had occupied much of north-eastern and eastern China, and each other. After the Japanese defeat, the Communists, led by Mao Zedong, drove out their bitter rivals, the Nationalists, or Kuomintang, forcing them to flee to the island of Taiwan. China still claims Taiwan as a province, even though the island has its own government.

Female workers at a crockery packaging factory in Guangzhou. Compared to Europe and the USA, labour costs in China are low so its goods are highly competitive in the world market. ▼

Chinese economy

To rebuild China's economy, shattered by years of war, the Communists organized farms into cooperatives and brought industry under state control. But they suffered major setbacks with the failure of the economic plan called the 'Great Leap Forward' (1958–60), which caused food shortages and halved industrial output.

The policy of 'Cultural Revolution', launched by Mao Zedong in 1966, also turned out badly. It started a wave of attacks on politicians by young Red Guards, and sometimes the army was called in to restore order.

Since Mao's death in 1976, the Chinese government has reduced support for state-owned industries, allowed some private companies to set up, and opened up its markets to foreign trade so as to gain entry to the World Trade Organization. By 1999, China had the fastest-growing economy in the world, and in 2002 the growth in its gross domestic product – a measure of economic performance – reached 8 per cent, four times higher than in 1978.

Web Search ▶▶

▶ http://www.china.org.cn/e-china/history/index.htm
China in Brief *articles on all periods of Chinese history from the official standpoint.*

▶ http://china.9c9c.com/History/
Short articles on the history of China from ancient to modern times.

▶ http://www.economist.co.uk/countries/china/
Economist *magazine page devoted to China with links to factsheet, forecast and other pages.*

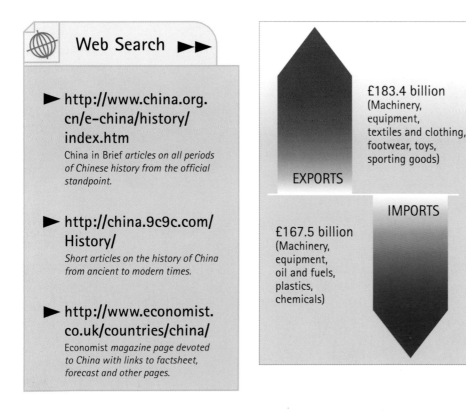

£183.4 billion
(Machinery, equipment, textiles and clothing, footwear, toys, sporting goods)

EXPORTS

IMPORTS

£167.5 billion
(Machinery, equipment, oil and fuels, plastics, chemicals)

DATABASE

Chronology of Historical Events: 1945 to present-day

1945 Japanese defeat in World War II leaves Kuomintang and Communists fighting each other

1949
Final victory for the Communists under Mao Zedong, who proclaims the People's Republic of China. Chiang Kai-shek escapes to Taiwan

1958–60
Great Leap Forward. Optimistic reorganization of agriculture and industry leads to famine, killing millions

1966–76
Cultural Revolution, involving hounding of Mao's political opponents

1971
China admitted to the United Nations in place of Taiwan

1976
Death of Mao Zedong

1978
Deng Xiaoping emerges as leader and introduces 'Four Modernizations', in agriculture, industry, the armed forces and technology

1997
Hong Kong, a former British colony, and, in 1999, Macau, a former Portuguese territory, returned to China

2002
China joins World Trade Organization

◀◀ China enjoys a balance of trade surplus, that is, the value of the goods exported by China exceeds the value of the goods that it imports. China's chief trading partners are the USA, Japan, South Korea, Taiwan and European Union countries.

Area:
9,596,960 sq km

Population size:
1.29 billion

Capital city:
Beijing (population 13.82 million)

Other major cities:
Shanghai (16.74 million), Guangzhou (10.15 million), Tianjin (10.01 million), Chengdu (9.97 million)

Longest river:
Changjiang (Yangtse) (6,300 km)

Highest mountain:
Mount Everest (Qomolangma) (8,848 m)

Currency:
Renminbi (RMB) or yuan

Flag:
The flag was adopted in 1949 as the national flag of the People's Republic of China. Red stands for revolution. The largest star represents the Chinese Communist Party and its leadership. The four stars grouped around it represent the Chinese people.

Languages:
Official language: Putonghua (Mandarin Chinese)

Natural resources:
Coal, oil, natural gas, iron ore, tin, tungsten, salt, aluminium, nickel, lead, zinc, gold, copper, silver

Major exports:
Machinery, electrical equipment, oil, computers, cotton, silk, clothing, toys, shoes, sports goods, coal, cement, tea, soya

Main festivals and holidays:
End of January/start of February: The new year according to the Chinese lunar calendar. New Year's Day is a public holiday. Family get-togethers, fairs and lantern and flower parades all feature in a festival that lasts two weeks.
1 May: International Labour Day, a public holiday.
1 June: Children's Day. Schools take the children on trips to sites of cultural or historic interest.

August/September: Ghost Festival, in the seventh lunar month, when restless spirits of the dead are released from hell and families visit graves to pay their respects. Not considered a good time to travel, move house or get married.
September/October: Moon Festival/Mid-autumn Festival, celebrated on 15th day of the eighth lunar month. Family reunions to eat 'moon cakes' (sweet biscuits symbolizing family unity) and enjoy fireworks and lantern displays.
1 October: National Day. A public holiday to celebrate the anniversary of the founding of the People's Republic in 1949.

Official religion: None

Other religions:
Confucian 20 per cent, Buddhist 6 per cent, Muslim 2 per cent, Christian 1 per cent, traditional beliefs and others 12 per cent

Glossary

BALANCE OF TRADE
The value of the goods that a country sells to other countries (exports) minus the value of the goods purchased from other countries (imports). If the result is a plus figure, this is a balance of trade 'surplus'. If it is a minus figure, it is a balance of trade 'deficit'.

CALLIGRAPHY
The art of using brushes dipped in special inks to write Chinese characters.

COMMUNIST PARTY
A political party that bases its ideas of society on the theories of the German philosopher Karl Marx (1818–83). Communists believe in the common ownership of property, agriculture and industry. In practice, this has often turned out as tight government control by a one-party state.

CONFUCIANISM
A philosophy based on the teachings of the Chinese scholar Confucius, who was born in the 6th century BCE. He stressed good behaviour and honesty as the key to an orderly society.

CONSTITUTION
A list of principles, drawn up by a state, that sets out the powers and duties of the government and the rights and freedoms of the people.

ECONOMY
The basis on which a country's wealth is organized.

FENG SHUI
An ancient art based on the belief of order in the universe and the power of nature. Traditional Chinese homes are built and arranged according to its principles.

GROSS DOMESTIC PRODUCT (GDP)
The total value of the goods and services that a country produces. It is usually measured over a year or longer

MARTIAL ARTS
Sports, such as kung fu, based on traditional fighting methods, whether unarmed combat or fighting with weapons.

NATIONALITY
A group of people with a common language, culture or racial background.

PLATEAU
A large area of fairly flat, high ground.

PUTONGHUA
The official form of spoken Chinese, as it is spoken in Beijing. Also called Mandarin.

REPUBLIC
A country that is not ruled by a king or emperor, but has a president or elected leader as its head of state.

STEPPE
An extensive, treeless, grassy plain, found in Mongolia and Russia.

TAOISM
Philosophy and religion based on the teachings of Lao-tzu, who lived in the 6th century BCE. Taoists believe in the Tao, or 'way', whose object is to gain wisdom and create harmony.

TYPHOON
A violent, spiralling wind, in tropical climates, that comes off the ocean and can cause devastation when it hits land. It is also called a hurricane or cyclone.

UNITED NATIONS (UN)
An international organization, set up after World War II (1939–45), to foster world peace and good relations between all countries.

UNITED NATIONS (UN) SECURITY COUNCIL
The UN body responsible for maintaining peace and order between countries. China, the USA, Russia, the UK and France are the five permanent members. Ten other member countries are elected to serve for two years. A permanent member of the Council has the power to block any proposal for action that it does not agree with.

WARLORD
The leader of an armed group who controls an area or region by use of force and terror.

YURT
The traditional Mongolian home, consisting of a circular felt or hide tent stretched over a wooden framework. It could quickly be dismantled and assembled, so that the Mongolian herders could move on to new pastures for their flocks.

Index